Quaker Roots and Branches

From his insight that modern day Quakers are the product and carriers of an inspiring tradition, John Lampen paints a compelling picture of the Quaker character: clear intellectual enquiry, resolute moral integrity, and quiet, unsung heroism. The lives he describes are led by the guidance emerging from silent worship. In describing the resonance of these Quaker lives with his personal experience, John makes these stories relevant for us today.

Gerald Hewitson, Author, *Journey into Life: Inheriting The Story of Early Friends*

This exploration of Quaker identity shows how modern Quaker ways have developed out of, but are clearly rooted in, the lives of earlier generations. It is engaging and very readable. John Lampen gives frequent examples of real Quakers seeking to follow 'guidance'. There are some familiar stories, and some quite tantalising glimpses into less well-known characters which left me wanting to know more. They illustrate how today's Quaker practice is frequently on a continuum with the past, but at other times breaks significantly with tradition – and it is helpful to be aware of which is which, and why. A worthwhile read for anyone wanting to understand early 21st century (British) Quakers!

Helen Rowlands, former Head of Education, Woodbrooke Quaker Study Centre, Birmingham, UK

John Lampen has a gift for connecting the contemporary concerns of Friends with the rich heritage of the Quaker past. In his latest collection of essays, he shows us how the experiences of Friends like George Fox, William Penn, and Elizabeth Fry offer us wisdom and guidance in confronting the problems we face today.

Thomas Hamm, Professor of History, Earlham College, Richmond, Indiana, U.S.A.

QUAKER QUICKS

Quaker Roots and Branches

WITHDRAWN

Quaker Quicks is a new series from Christian Alternative focusing upon aspects of Quaker faith and theology. Beginning with *Quaker Roots and Branches* the series will build into a valuable resource both for Quakers and those interested in this unique expression of belief, practice and theology. Watch out for upcoming titles on Quaker theology, faith and practice, and studies in social aspects such as economics and pacifism.

QUAKER QUICKS

Quaker Roots and Branches

John Lampen

CHRISTIAN
ALTERNATIVE

Winchester, UK
Washington, USA

First published by Christian Alternative Books, 2018
Christian Alternative Books is an imprint of John Hunt Publishing Ltd.,
No. 3 East St., Alresford, Hampshire SO24 9EE, UK
office1@jhpbooks.net
www.johnhuntpublishing.com
www.christian-alternative.com

For distributor details and how to order please visit the 'Ordering' section on our website.

Text copyright: John Lampen 2017
Cover photo: Quaker Climate Justice protest at the British Museum

ISBN: 978 1 78535 834 0
978 1 78535 841 8 (ebook)
Library of Congress Control Number: 2017953307

A CIP catalogue record for this book is available from the British Library.

Design: Stuart Davies

Printed and bound by CPI Group (UK) Ltd, Croydon, CR0 4YY, UK
US: Printed and bound by Edwards Brothers Malloy 15200 NBN Way #B, Blue Ridge Summit, PA 17214, USA

We operate a distinctive and ethical publishing philosophy in all areas of our business, from our global network of authors to production and worldwide distribution.

Contents

Introduction   1

The Environment   3

War and Peace   15

Punishment   24

The Arts, Especially Music   38

Experience, Belief and Theology   48

Glossary   61

Introduction

When people have heard of Quakers at all, their picture is often based on our past. We are sometimes told, "I didn't know Quakers still existed!" Beyond images of a peculiar dress code and puritan attitudes to enjoying ourselves, they may have a hazy impression of the Quaker refusal to fight, or our influence on ending the slave trade and reforming Victorian prisons, or just chocolate manufacture; and in Ireland there are memories of our relief work during the Great Hunger and the modern Troubles.

In contrast, within the Society of Friends in Britain I think the picture we have of ourselves does not take sufficient account of our history. In our key document, *Quaker Faith & Practice*, the great majority of the quotations come from the 20th century; and most of the earlier ones are from the first fifty years of our existence. Stories which we used to tell our children are forgotten. Friends (as we call ourselves) often seem uncomfortable about our forebears: their evangelical fervour, their apparent intolerance of other people's beliefs, their certainty that they were right, and their claim to discern and embody "the will of God".

I think this disconnection is a misunderstanding and a pity; the continuity is more important than the differences. I think we could help Quakers become more certain of their identity if they had a clearer picture of how our community has been evolving over three hundred and sixty five years; and it would help others to know how we are the product and the carriers of an inspiring tradition.

Quaker witness, or what we call our testimonies*, is based not on rules but on guidelines which evolve continually. What comes first is either the pressing awareness of a problem, or an inspiration to act in a certain way, sometimes unexpectedly. The action may seem absurd or counter-productive; but it has a

1

compelling quality. Later we may come to an understanding of why it was right to undertake it. I know that we have often been fallible, but both mistakes and achievements can be revealing. However, if we are to understand the relevance of our past we must learn to translate some older forms of language and thought. In this short book, I have chosen five areas which matter to Friends and other people today to show the paths we have taken.

I have added a short glossary of words which Quakers use in a special sense, based on *Quakerspeak* by my dear friend Alastair Heron.

* Indicates that a term is explained in the glossary at the end of the book

The Environment

In 2011 Quakers in Britain made a commitment to become a low-carbon, sustainable community, living out this promise in their personal lives and as a faith community. They began campaigning for climate and energy justice, and to build a fairer economy which is not powered by fossil fuels. We tend to think of this as a recent concern*, but much of it goes back to our origins. It is something like a jigsaw, for which earlier generations fashioned the pieces. Now modern science has documented the connections between things which we used to address separately. We can see a larger picture as the pieces are put together.

The Natural World

George Fox, the founder of the Quaker movement, says that as a child of eleven he realised "that I might not eat and drink to make myself wanton but for health, using the [animal and vegetable] creatures... as servants in their places, to the glory of him who hath created them." Later mystical experiences convinced him that he was a part of the whole natural world. He sensed he was given an intuitive knowledge of the nature and virtues of plants, and wondered if he was destined to take up medicine. Later, when Quakers began to found schools, he asked for them to have herb gardens, to instruct the boys and girls in "whatsoever things were civil and useful in the creation."

This sense of unity with the creation was part of the original Quaker vision, shared by many of his comrades. They saw it as part of God's bounty to humanity and were deeply concerned that we should not abuse it. George Fox criticised the rich as "madmen that destroy the creation and the creatures of God upon your lusts!" And William Penn wrote: "The world represents a rare and sumptuous palace, mankind the great family in it...

3

the heavens adorned with so many glorious luminaries; and the earth with groves, plains, valleys, hills, fountains, ponds, lakes and rivers; and a variety of fruits and creatures for food, pleasure and profit. In short, how noble a house [God] keeps, and the plenty and variety and excellency of his table: his order and seasons, and suitableness of every time and thing. But we must be as sensible... what careless and idle servants we are, and how short and disproportionate our behaviour is to his bounty and goodness."

A century later in America John Woolman reverenced nature, working in his orchard and urging us not to "lessen that sweetness of life in the animal creation, which the great Creator intends for them under our government." Nature's balance demonstrated God's intention for us. Perhaps he had learnt from the Native Americans he met that if we take from nature what we need, it renews itself; but if we take more, we destroy it, and that is a theft from our descendants. He showed how the economics of greed distorted the human environment too by diverting the efforts of poorer men into producing unnecessary and indeed harmful goods, which they could not afford to enjoy themselves. He urged a moral solution: to open ourselves to the love which had provided such bounty and intended it for all. "Divine love imposeth no rigorous or unreasonable commands, but graciously points out the spirit of brotherhood and way to happiness." This can only be found when "we go forth out of all that is selfish."

One of the things which struck Thomas Clarkson, the British hero of the anti-slavery movement and a sympathetic observer of Quakers, was their kindness to their own animals. He mentions their aversion to hunting, hawking and shooting because of the cruelty involved. At a time when such ideas were almost unknown, "Quakers are of opinion that rights and duties have sprung up — rights on behalf of animals and duties on the part of men — and that breach of these duties, however often or however

4

thoughtlessly it takes place, is a breach of a moral law."

Quaker Science: Medicine

Arthur Raistrick wrote that in the 17th century, "Alongside the religious questings and searchings out of which Quakerism emerged there was an ever-increasing urge to explore and to understand the physical world and its implications. There was a new acceptance of the function of observation and experiment in the search… It was impossible for people endowed with the active, enquiring spirit characteristic of Friends, keenly alive to the unity of life and dedicated… to the searching out and love of truth, to stand apart…" Scientific enquiry was another part of the jigsaw. Friends saw the natural world as a lesson in God's love for us. Science was an innocent pursuit which would bring benefit, not harm, to humankind.

"The Seed" was a favourite Quaker metaphor for "that of God in us". Inspired by Jesus' parables, Friends were impressed by the life hidden in seeds which has the power to burst out and grow, but depends on our planting and nurturing. So botany became a favourite Quaker science. Thomas Lawson, one of the early Quaker travelling missionaries, pursued George Fox's interest in the virtues of plants. At the very start of systematic botany, he recorded and described over four hundred different species. Many Friends followed him, writing to one another across the oceans and inventing the systematic taxonomy of British and American flora. Several of them corresponded with the great Swedish naturalist Linnaeus, exchanged ideas and sent him plants. The Quaker botanists saw the richness of the kingdom of plants as evidence of the power and wisdom of God; they would have been horrified at the accelerating loss of species today as a result of human activity.

George Fox drew attention to the curative properties of herbs, and many of the Quaker botanists followed him, with a number of distinguished contributions to biology and medicine.

They combined their fascination with nature with their wish to serve people, following the example of Jesus as a healer and witnessing to humanity's unity with the world of nature. Among the Quaker doctors were Thomas Hodgkin (after whom a disease is named) and John Lettsom. In the next generation Joseph Lister the founder of antiseptic surgery was raised a Quaker. But my hero is John Fothergill, who qualified as a doctor in 1740.

He was a man of very wide interests. He based his work on continual close observation of his patients, rather than following the orthodoxies of the time. He pioneered the use of simple prescriptions such as quinine in place of the unresearched compounds of his day based on superstition and alchemy (horse dung was a common ingredient!) He only gave drugs to patients as part of a holistic course of treatment. He urged the contribution of good diet, fresh air and exercise to the healing process. In 1749 he became famous for stemming an epidemic of scarlet fever among children in London, refusing to bleed his patients and giving them one single medicine supported by diet, cleanliness and good nursing. He could then have become rich by devoting himself to a wealthy clientèle; instead he continued his work among the poor and his researches into diseases which were untreatable at the time, including epilepsy, syphilis and sciatica. He did the first systematic research into the symptoms and treatment of influenza. He pioneered a regime to help women come through the menopause, with attention to its psychological concomitants. He set up Medical Societies which met regularly to listen to papers and discuss treatments. John Lettsom and he supported Jenner (not a Quaker) in his work on vaccination and helped establish the practice across Britain and the American colonies. They investigated accounts of the resuscitation of people who had almost drowned, and Lettsom founded the Royal Humane Society to set up first aid posts and train workers in these methods.

John Fothergill kept a large botanical garden to support his research into new medicines. He financed the illustrations to Linnaeus' great book, *The Sexual System of Plants*. He encouraged Benjamin Franklin in his electrical experiments and helped to get them published. These two friends tried to prevent war between Britain and its American colonies as we shall see later. Fothergill welcomed John Woolman to London and supported schemes for the emancipation of slaves.

It was noticeable that most Quaker doctors followed Fothergill's example of not running after wealthy clients. Many of them worked free of charge among the poor. Quaker chemists developed dispensaries in slum districts offering cheap pure medicines. These Friends also took an interest in public health, advocating for fresh air, nourishing food, good hygiene and sea bathing. Around forty years before Elizabeth Fry's first prison visit, John Lettsom was visiting prisons regularly, bringing large quantities of medicines and good food, and persuading both staff and prisoners of the importance of cleanliness. Their stories give the lie to the idea that eighteenth-century Quakers formed an inward-looking society, with little interest in the needs of the wider world.

Quaker Science: Physics

Other Quaker scientists contributed to the jigsaw through the pure pursuit of knowledge. I have no space to mention them all, but Raistrick wrote that "Friends have secured something like forty times their due proportion of Fellows of the Royal Society during its long history." The tradition has continued in the twentieth century with scientists like Kathleen Lonsdale, who did pioneering work in x-rays and crystals (and went to prison in 1943 as a conscientious objector), and Jocelin Bell Burnell, the discoverer of radio pulsars. I will pick out two earlier Friends because they were outstanding in their fields, one dealing with the tiny components of nature, the other with its grandest aspect.

John Dalton did important research in meteorology and

colour-blindness (from which he suffered) but he is chiefly famous as the author of the modern atomic theory and discoverer of "atomic weights" (1807). He endorsed what John Woolman had concluded about the world we inhabit: "We should scarcely be excused in concluding this essay without calling the reader's attention to the beneficent and wise laws established by the Author of nature to provide for the various exigencies of the sublunary creation, and to make the several parts dependent upon each other, so as to form one well-regulated system or whole" —an anticipation of the Gaia hypothesis.

Arthur Eddington became Professor of Astronomy and Experimental Philosophy at Cambridge in 1913. He made crucial contributions to the understanding of stars. As secretary of the Royal Astronomical Society during the War, he was the first to hear about Einstein's theory of general relativity. He was one of the few astronomers with the mathematical skills to understand it; and with his Quakerly internationalist and pacifist outlook he was rare among British scientists in being willing to pursue a theory developed by a German physicist. He became the chief supporter and advocate of the theory in Britain.

When conscription was introduced Eddington claimed conscientious objector status, making clear his willingness to serve at the Front in the Friends Ambulance Unit, or as a harvest labourer. His application was not granted. The Astronomer Royal, Sir Frank Dyson, supported Eddington at a later hearing, emphasising Eddington's essential role in the solar eclipse expedition planned for May 1919. The tribunal granted him twelve months' exemption from military service on condition that he continued his scientific work. His observations during the expedition to Principe provided the first proof that Einstein's theory was correct.

Eddington compared his studies and his faith during his Swarthmore Lecture* to the 1929 Quaker Yearly Meeting*: "We have no creed in science, but we are not lukewarm in our beliefs... not that all the knowledge of the universe which we hold so enthusiastically will survive in the letter; but a sureness that we are on the road... So too in religion we are repelled by that confident theological doctrine which has settled for all generations just how the spiritual world is worked; but we need not turn aside from the measure of light that comes into our experience showing us a Way through the unseen world... There is a kind of sureness which is very different from cocksureness."

The inspiration of all the Friends who so studied and loved the natural world was well expressed by Sarah Baker, a lecturer in botanical chemistry in University College, London, in 1912, when such posts rarely went to women, and a trained artist. She died five years later at the age of twenty-nine. Her Sunday School class recalled her telling them "that the universe is always singing, while only man is silent; and that man must learn to listen, so that his heart may join the universal chorus."

The Human Environment

George Fox, William Penn and, later, John Woolman all said that the personal spiritual life, the human community and the natural world are interdependent, just as the pieces of a jigsaw link together. Violence to any one damages them all. Fox wrote: "You merchants, great men and rich men, what a dishonour is it to you to go in your gold and silver, and gold chains about your necks and your costly attire, and your poor, blind women and children, and cripples, crying and making a noise up and down your streets... How can you go up and down in your superfluity, and abounding in your riches, and see the poor, blind, and cripples go about your streets?"

John Woolman's concerns for the welfare of the natural world and of human society were inseparable. He objected to inequality of labour even more than inequality of income, because he saw that the huge demands put on working people damaged their health, their chance to contribute to the affairs of society,

9

and their spiritual lives. This was caused by the conspicuous consumption of the rich. Slavery exacerbated the problem, and he argued against it on economic and moral grounds: "Were all superfluities and the desire of outward greatness left aside, and the right use of things universally attended to, such a number of people might be employed in things useful that moderate labour with the blessing of heaven would answer all good purposes relating to people and their animals." Slavery of course was the extreme example of inequality, and Quakers were at the forefront of efforts to eliminate it.

Quakers involved in the new industries of the nineteenth century found Woolman's advice harder to follow, and some of them became very wealthy. But the Yearly Meeting strongly counselled them against speculation, living beyond their means, or adopting a lavish lifestyle. (Quite a number of business men indeed found the discipline too strict, and left the Society of Friends.) Quaker employers felt a responsibility to the community from which their workers came. When the chocolate manufacturers became aware of the slum homes of their workers, they were horrified; they felt an immediate need to create healthy and attractive living spaces for them, with decent housing, good schools, community buildings, parks, libraries, sports fields and swimming pools, and tree-lined roads. The innovation was widely admired and followed. In this way the Quaker concern with public health and preventative medicine which began with John Fothergill and his friends persisted into the twentieth century.

Alfred Salter was another Quaker doctor who could have had a brilliant career in research. But his daily journey through London as a medical student had shown him the slums of Bermondsey, where five families might live in a single room, and one water closet serve twenty-five houses. He decided that his life work must be there. In 1900 he rented a corner shop as his clinic, and became a local councillor (and later a Member of Parliament). From this base he struggled for better housing, better health care and an environment rich in trees and flowers. His wife Ada was also elected to the local council and engaged in parallel work, particularly with girls at risk. She became the Mayor of Bermondsey, the first female Mayor in London, and the first Labour Party female Mayor anywhere. By the 1930s she had planted 7000 trees in the Borough, decorated buildings with window-boxes, and filled all open spaces with flowers. She provided music concerts, art competitions, games, sports and children's playgrounds. The council houses built under her leadership are still cited today as an exceptional example of public housing.

Contemporary Concerns

Though Quakers achieved so much in these areas of environmental concern, it was others who connected the different strands and inspired the present Quaker concern for the sustainability of our planet. There were three books which shocked me and my generation into understanding how and why the world was going wrong and how it needed to change. The first was Rachel Carson's *The Silent Spring* in 1962, showing us how we were poisoning our planet. Then in 1973 E. F. Schumacher published *Small is Beautiful: a study of economics as if people mattered*, which was an attack on the unquestioned notion of limitless technological progress. At the end of that decade James Lovelace wrote *Gaia–A New Look at Life on Earth*, a vision of our planet as a single self-regulating system, endangered by our reckless behaviour and our inability to understand its complexity.

These books contributed vital pieces to the jigsaw. They helped us to integrate the earlier Quaker experiences and understand where they had been pointing us. Aspects of these writers' work may have been attacked, even discredited, but it is clear that their overall message is true and many besides Friends have been hearing it.

The world and humanity are in deep trouble. The symptoms are undeniable, among them pollution, drought and floods, local conflicts over vanishing resources (especially water), the depletion of fossil fuels and other mineral reserves, migration forced by wars and desertification, poverty within affluent societies, the increase of cancer, and mounting rubbish (some of it toxic). The immediate causes are becoming clear too, including climate change, the loss of food production because of soil erosion, cash cropping and ill-conceived farming processes, the employment of science to boost consumerism and the means of warfare, and inequality of income in both rich and poor societies. But Quakers believe that the underlying causes are spiritual: a culture strong in greed and weak on compassion, a failure in long-term vision, and a misunderstanding of the sources of happiness. John Woolman wrote in 1772, "So great is the hurry in the spirit of this world that in aiming to do business quick and to gain wealth, the creation at this day doth loudly groan."

So Quakers are learning what our testimonies to simplicity of life, equality and justice should mean in today's world. They find themselves, thankfully, as a small part of a much bigger movement. So is there anything that they in particular can contribute? George Fox advised Friends to be patterns and examples in the world; even if we are too few to change the spirit of the age, many Friends are living in a way which shows that there can be an alternative. They ensure their homes and Meeting Houses do not waste energy, they reduce their air travel, they become vegetarian, they recycle materials, they do not chase after the newest gadget when the one they have serves them well enough. They invoke the Quaker peace testimony and bear witness to the fact that the immediate consequences of the crisis are hurting other people much less able to protect themselves than we are. Climate change results in wars, drought, sickness and the displacement of peoples, causing enormous misery. It is not only nature but humankind who are suffering. And it is our "western" society which is causing it.

When they cannot solve a huge problem, Quakers use their worship to discern what each of them is guided to do about it. (I will look at what we mean by guidance* in the final chapter of this book.) Instead of being overwhelmed by hopelessness, we can take up one task and make some contribution to change, relying on others to work on other parts of the problem. Many Friends are doing so, and some of this work has been taken up by larger Quaker bodies. To give two examples: the Quaker United Nations Office* in Geneva has been supporting poor farmers in developing countries by bringing together representatives of governments and making them more aware of small-scale farmers' and other stakeholders' experience, skills and interests in relation to intellectual property discussions that affect agriculture. These include attempts by multinational companies to acquire patents of the genomes of plants which the farmers use. They are looking at the effects of outside interventions on indigenous communities from a human rights standpoint, and commissioning research about different approaches to the intellectual property protection of seeds and genetic resources.

Secondly, Quakers in Britain were the first church in Britain to divest our centrally held money from fossil fuels. Local and Area Quaker Meetings* are now doing the same. They thus question the morality of the fossil fuel industry, and challenge its power. They campaign for justice for those who have been unequally impacted by climate change and call for global climate action that stops this injustice continuing. They say, "We think all people have the right to affordable energy that does not harm the planet. We want an end to fuel poverty. We believe there should be more equality in the way energy is owned and organised. We want an end to dominance of the energy system by big companies and an increase in community ownership."

Despite the diversity in our tradition over the centuries, when the pieces are fitted together the jigsaw shows a single picture. It says that caring for our planet is a spiritual concern: it is not just about our material wellbeing and the welfare of our descendants. To live responsibly and unselfishly is essential to our spiritual health.

Further Reading

Arthur Eddington: *Science and the Unseen World* (Swarthmore Lecture, 1929)

Grigor McClelland: *And a New Earth: Making Tomorrow's Society Better Than Today's* (Swarthmore Lecture, 1976)

Pam Lunn: *Costing not less than everything: Sustainability and spirituality in challenging times*

(Swarthmore Lecture, 2011)

War and Peace

Two of the United Nation's achievements in the last fifty years were the prohibitions on the recruitment and use of child soldiers (now included in the Geneva Conventions on War and the Convention on the Rights of the Child) and the Convention on the Prohibition of the Use, Stockpiling, Production and Transfer of Anti-Personnel Mines and on Their Destruction. Both of these have been accepted by the great majority of nations. The Quaker Offices at the United Nations* played a vital role in raising awareness of the issues and persuading governments to support the changes. What is the link between that work and a lonely 27-year-old in a seventeenth century English gaol, refusing to be released when the price was for him to join the army?

Refusing to Fight

That prisoner was George Fox, the first Quaker. He said that every person has something of God in them, and that this teaches them how to live. He realised this without any help from the bible, though he later found confirmation there. In his terms, what the Inward Christ taught him directly agreed with what the historical Christ had said. In the specific case of war, his contemporary Robert Barclay put the argument forcefully: "Whoever can reconcile this, *Resist not evil,* with *Resist violence by force,* again, *Give also thy other cheek* with *Strike again;* also, *Love thine enemies* with *Spoil them, make a prey of them, pursue them with fire and the sword,* or *Pray for those that persecute you and those that calumniate you* with *Persecute them with fines, imprisonment and death itself,* whoever, I say, can find a means to reconcile these things may be supposed also to have found a way to reconcile God with the Devil."

George Fox did not try to impose this view on other Friends, many of whom came from the army. The conviction that fighting

15

was wrong gradually spread among them, till in 1660 Quakers produced a manifesto which said "We utterly deny all outward wars and strife with outward weapons for any end... The Spirit of Christ, which leads us into all truth, will never move us to fight and war against any man... neither for the kingdom of Christ, nor for the kingdoms of this world." George Fox saw clearly that it was a personal obligation on Friends to live peaceably; but he did not oppose them watching with their neighbours against lawbreakers as long as they did not carry weapons, nor reporting criminals to the magistrates to get them punished. His own endurance of violent attacks on him and his forgiveness afterwards bore impressive witness to his belief in nonviolence. He also foreshadowed later Quaker practice in mediation: "And so we went again to our inn, and there were two desperate fellows fighting so that none durst come nigh to part them; but I was moved in the Lord's power to go to them, and when I had loosed their hands I held one by one hand and one by the other hand; and I showed them the evil of their doings and convinced them, and reconciled them to each other that they were loving and very thankful..."

Since then individual Friends have occasionally decided that they have no alternative in conscience to taking up arms; many did in 1914. But in general they have undergone considerable suffering rather than fight. The Quaker conviction to refuse to fight, and to suffer for it rather than compromise, persuaded the British parliament to acknowledge the right to conscientious objection when they introduced conscription in 1916, even though this was an unpopular concession.

Friends still support everyone's right to refuse to go to war. We don't have conscription in Britain today but Friends House Moscow works with Russian conscientious objectors. The same belief inspired the concern about the use of child soldiers. There is also a dilemma about paying taxes used to prepare for war. Quakers in 18th-century Pennsylvania and elsewhere sometimes took the option of paying for a soldier to serve in their place. But John Woolman felt that doing so we were gradually becoming "a peaceable people" in name only. He and some others suffered their goods to be distrained rather than willingly financing war. This takes a modern form in the parliamentary campaign called *Conscience* to allow us to divert that portion of tax which is dedicated to "defence" to peaceful and socially useful purposes instead. *Conscience* was started and supported by British Quakers.

The Relief of Suffering

Refusing to fight (particularly if one willingly pays war taxes) invites the accusation that the pacifist is a coward sheltering behind the weapons of others. Peter the Great of Russia said testily to a Quaker in 1698, "Of what use can you be in any kingdom or government, seeing you will not bear arms and fight?" Friends respond to a deeply challenging issue of this kind by being open to guidance in the meeting for worship*. Guidance often begins with the insight of one Friend, (as the concern for child soldiers did) which is recognised by other Friends as what we call a "leading"*. In 1755 Anthony Benezet in Philadelphia encouraged his Meeting to support a group of war refugees. Over the next century there were similar efforts in other wars, instigated by individual groups of Friends. But in the Franco-Prussian War of 1870-1, the British and Irish Yearly Meetings set up a War Victims Relief Committee which raised £162,000 to help noncombatants, and sent forty-one commissioners to France and Germany to distribute it. Their efforts were poorly co-ordinated and inefficient; but this was one of the first initiatives of this kind, which paved the way for the professional relief agencies of today.

The War Victims Relief Committee was revived in 1914, and at first worked mainly in France, helping refugees and running a maternity hospital close to the front line. In 1916 it sent missions to Serbia and Russia, where their work continued after the war.

There was terrible famine in Russia, and Friends had to win the trust and co-operation of the new Soviet authorities. After the armistice they also provided relief in the countries which Britain had been fighting, Germany and Austria. In post-war Vienna, Dr Hilda Clarke distributed food and clothing to 10,000 children, reopened hospitals, bought cattle to provide milk, and obtained land where hundreds of displaced people could build their own houses; it is one of the great and almost forgotten Quaker stories. During and after the 1939-45 War this Committee, renamed the Friends Relief Service, was active again and working in almost as many countries.

The Friends Ambulance Unit (FAU) was also set up in 1914. It was never an official Quaker organisation, and many of its 1700 members were not Friends. Conscientious objectors serving with the Unit did not have to face tribunals when conscription came in. They were people who wanted to support their country in its struggle and take the same risks as the soldiers though without killing. Twenty one of them died on active service. They worked in Britain, France and Belgium, in hospitals, ambulance trains and ships. The FAU was revived in the Second World War with 1314 members (of whom 97 were women). Seventeen were killed, a higher death rate proportionally than in the army during most of the war. As Ormerod Greenwood wrote, "Units found themselves in the freezing Arctic forests of the north of Finland, in the desert sands of Tobruk and Alamein, in the malaria-ridden villages of Syria, in hospitals in the mountainous capital of Ethiopia. They experienced the perilous convoys of the Burma Road; they served in famine-stricken India; and they followed in the wake of the invading armies into Italy, the Balkans, the Dodecanese, north-west Europe and Austria." There is no better evidence that a pacifist need not be a coward.

The existence of "official" Quaker relief work did not mean the end of individual initiatives. Oxfam, for example, arose from the wish of a small group, mostly Quaker, in 1942 to respond to the famine in Greece caused by Nazi occupation and the Allied blockade. They lobbied the government to let food ships through; when this was refused they raised £10,000 for the Greek Red Cross and managed to get food supplies into the country.

Sometimes previous Quaker relief work has paved the way for later efforts at reconciliation. The feeding and reconstruction in Austria and Germany after 1919 opened doors to Friends in Berlin in the 1930s. Quaker Centres in the Northern Irish prisons ministered to political prisoners and their families on both sides of the conflict, giving credibility to those Friends who quietly facilitated dialogue among their leaders and between them and the British authorities.

Removing the Causes of War: Reconciliation

The effects of refusing to fight and organising relief in wartime are only felt after the violence has begun. This has troubled Quakers, and it gradually became clear to them that rather than wait for wars to start they should try to prevent them and remove their causes, and to mediate between parties in conflict. This is often seen as a modern practice, but John Fothergill worked with Benjamin Franklin in 1774 to agree on seventeen points to be submitted to the British government to avoid an American war of independence. Sadly, these were rejected.

Quakers later made contact with Czar Alexander I to urge a peaceful stance during the negotiations after the Napoleonic Wars; he was impressed with those he met and asked for a Quaker to be sent to oversee the draining of the marshes round St Petersburg. When pressure was growing in Britain to fight with Turkey against Russia in the Crimean conflict in 1854, Friends renewed this connection by sending a peace deputation to the current Czar. They had an audience with him and were expecting a second one when political developments rendered their mission hopeless. They were ridiculed when they got home; but later, when the horrors of the Crimean War were reported there, their attempt was seen more favourably.

The devastation of the First World War brought the international community for the first time to create international institutions for peace (an idea first advocated by the Quakers William Penn and John Bellers in the seventeenth century). Quakers were enthusiastic advocates for the League of Nations and later the United Nations. Philip Noel-Baker, an Olympic silver medallist, Quaker and member of the FAU during the war, was closely involved in the formation of the League; and after the Second World War he helped as a British delegate to draft the constitution of the UN. He received the Nobel Peace Prize in 1959 for his work. Quakers have established Quaker United Nations Offices in New York and Geneva, to research issues, raise awareness, give national delegates opportunities for confidential discussion, and build consensus. The Conventions on Child Soldiers and on Landmines which I mentioned earlier were among their many achievements.

Between the two World Wars the Quaker Council for International Service ran seven Peace Embassies in major European cities to work unobtrusively for mutual understanding and the reduction of tension. These did not survive the war; but the same idea has been renewed in more recent times, in Quaker House Belfast, Friends House Moscow, and the Quaker Peace Centre in Cape Town, South Africa. Friends were involved as unofficial mediators in several major conflicts, such as the Nigerian civil war and the birth of Zimbabwe. Because they are not seeking praise and fame, and willingly work in co-operation with other peacemakers, their contributions are little known. As Mother Teresa said of her own work, they are "a drop in the ocean" of international conflicts, "but a drop which would be missed".

Removing the Causes of War: Peace Education

The UNESCO Constitution begins: "Since wars begin in the

minds of men, it is in the minds of men that the defences of peace must be constructed". But where to begin? By changing people's thinking, or their attitudes and behaviour? 20thcentury Quakers have contributed to both strategies.

Military history and the "science of war" are long-established academic disciplines. During the Cold War, British and American Friends began to realise it was equally important to create a science of peace: to understand how conflicts develop, why they sometimes turn violent, and how they can be resolved creatively and peacefully. It was hoped that rigorous thinking and research could begin to inform policy-makers. And indeed terms familiar to policy makers today, like "win-win solutions" and "zero-sum games" developed out of this thinking. In 1973 the Quaker Peace Studies Trust raised the money to endow the first Chair in Peace Studies in a British university, at Bradford. The professor was Adam Curle, a Quaker well-known for his peace-making in violent situations in Pakistan, Southern Africa and Nigeria.

Around the same time inmates of a New York prison asked local Quakers to develop a programme to help them not to give way to violence in situations of fear or provocation. The use of force had become a habitual reaction which damaged their personal and social relationships and put them in prison. The result was "Alternatives to Violence" (AVP), a programme which now operates in prisons and the wider community in more than fifty countries.

Soon some of the AVP pioneers turned their attention to children, reasoning that we could transform the world if the defences of peace were built in the mind at an early age. Children proved quick to learn the benefits of peace skills and creative problem solving, and to mediate their friends' conflicts. Quakers, working with other partners, have taken this idea around the world. It has proved particularly effective in societies in conflict. I took part in peace education workshops in Northern Ireland between Catholic and Protestant children who had never met before; and once we had a group of visitors from the Soviet Union who watched on closed-circuit television and later talked to the children. It was at the time when the Union was breaking up, and they were so impressed that they asked us to bring our methods to their countries.

Having worked in the field of peace education in many settings from kindergartens to universities, (including prisons), I have found that there is less gap than you might think between the academic and practical approaches. University peace studies do not explore remote and abstract concepts but the stuff of daily interactions between people, groups and nations, causing damage, distress and alienation. Stripped of the jargon, the question of why conflicts escalate and how the process can be reversed is as important to children and families as it is to academics. When I worked with very young children I was using the same ideas as I did when I wrote my MPhil thesis; I just had to find the right language and examples for a young audience. A prisoner once said to me, "If I had learnt this stuff as a kid, I wouldn't be here now!"

Endurance

Critics have described pacifism as an easy option; conscientious objectors were called "shirkers" and cowards in the First World War. But following the peace testimony may involve courage and considerable suffering. The early Friends found this in the days of persecution, as did the 1916 conscientious objectors who went to prison rather than accept any service which might assist the war effort. Other Quakers have endured harsh conditions in war, like the Norwegians who helped Jewish refugees to escape from the Nazis into neutral Sweden after 1940. I have space for two inspiring stories. In the American Civil War, three brothers refused to join the Confederate Army and were severely abused. Then "in the morning, when the order was given to march, William Hockett refused to take his place in the ranks.

This greatly exasperated the officer, who told him to prepare at once for death. Some soldiers were drawn up a few paces in front of him, and at the word of command they loaded and presented their guns. The meek and faithful Christian prayed, 'Father, forgive them for they know not what they do!' The guns dropped, and the men were heard to say that they could not shoot such a man."

The African-American Quaker Bayard Rustin co-founded the Southern Christian Leaders Conference with Martin Luther King. When King's house was bombed, he immediately obtained a gun and hired an armed guard. But Rustin convinced him that nonviolence had better resources than retaliation; but it obliged its followers to make themselves vulnerable. King got rid of the weapons. The patient endurance of unjust violence thus became the foundation of the Conference's initiatives, with a deeply persuasive effect on American public opinion.

The peace testimony is like a tree planted by the first Friends, which over time has formed three main stems: refusal to fight, binding up the wounds of war, and trying to remove its causes. We have seen that each of these stems has put out branches of its own, and all of them are still producing fruit today. We can picture the tree as being rooted in worship; we might think of the sap as being the inspiration which rises to nourish the leaves and fruit, but descends again to feed the roots with what it has gathered from the world outside.

For further reading

Adam Curle: *True Justice* (Swarthmore Lecture, 1981)
Diana Francis: *Faith, Power and Peace* (Swarthmore Lecture, 2015)
Esther Mombo and Cecile Nyiramana; *Mending broken hearts; rebuilding shattered lives - Quaker peace building in eastern Africa* (Swarthmore Lecture, 2016)

Punishment

Punishment is a concern that goes back to our earliest years. Today it has two branches. There are those who take their humanity and values into the prison system, working as staff or volunteers, or joining one of the pressure groups trying to change it. The other branch challenges the whole rationale of punishment, suggesting and sometimes trying out alternatives.

Quakers were well acquainted with prisons in the early days of persecution. They were imprisoned for breaking the law in such matters as not paying church tithes, refusing to take oaths, or contempt of court in not taking off their hats there. In a remarkable episode in 1659 a large group of Friends assembled in Westminster Hall and petitioned Parliament to take and imprison them, body for body, in the place of the 144 Friends then in prison. The appeal was rejected, but some of the prisoners were released.

Quakers pioneered what is now a common practice in direct action against unjust laws: to break the law in public, and willingly endure the legal penalty as a witness to its injustice. William Dewsbury, an ex-soldier from Yorkshire, said just before his death in 1688, "For I can say I never played the coward, but joyfully entered prisons as palaces, telling mine enemies to hold me there as long as they could: and in the prisonhouse I sung praises to my God and esteemed the bolts and locks put upon me as jewels..."

Friends were not only concerned for themselves. In his second imprisonment (out of eight), George Fox "was moved to write to the judges concerning their putting men to death for cattle and for money and for small things, several times, how contrary to the law of God it was." In 1682 William Penn who had also been imprisoned wrote: "We are too ready to retaliate, rather than forgive, or gain by Love and Information." In the same period

24

John Bellers proposed the total abolition of the death penalty and the transformation of prisons into places which took care of the offenders' wellbeing and gave them useful work to do, while helping them to reform. This was too radical to be considered at the time in England, but William Penn's *Frame of Government for Pennsylvania* rejected capital punishment for over two hundred offences for which it was used in England, keeping it only for murder.

The age of persecution passed, and Quakers became respectable, if eccentric. They became more preoccupied with their inner lives and their uniform lifestyle than with public affairs. But there were still individuals, like John Lettsom, the doctor mentioned earlier, who followed Jesus' teaching "I was in prison and you visited me." Friends whose faith led them into the world generally wanted to preach the gospel rather than to reform society, and some of them felt called to preach in prisons. Thomas Shillitoe gives an interesting account of his visit to Spandau prison in Germany, which shows the spirit in which such Friends proceeded.

Whilst walking along, I was accosted by my friend the chief magistrate of the city, saying, "So you are about to make another visit to Spandau. I would wish you not to go again. Are you not afraid? Don't you know some of the prisoners murdered the last governor?" Although I received his counsel as a mark of his kindness towards me... [it] caused me, for a time... to consider there was not only my own life, but that of my interpreter, the governor, and perhaps other attendants, at stake... These considerations, I found, without great watchfulness were in danger of producing such agitation of mind as would be very unprofitable for me.

I had concluded, in the course of the night previous to our proceeding to Spandau, to empty my pockets of money, watch, pocketbook, and my penknife more particularly; for, by having my penknife about me, I might be the cause of furnishing them with the means of my own destruction; this I accordingly did. But on mature deliberation on the step I had thus taken, I was mercifully led to see that it was the effect of that departure from a full and entire reliance on God's arm of power, which the enemy [Satan] was endeavouring to bring about in my mind... I, therefore, returned to my chamber, and replaced each of these articles as they were before, taking particular care that my penknife was not left behind.

He preached two sermons to the prisoners which were well received. In the first, entitled *Your Condition is not Hopeless*, he urged them to "be kindly disposed one to another, and regard not one another for evil."

In 1797 a revolutionary Quaker insight about punishment arose not from imprisonment but mental illness. Friends had established a mental hospital in York called the Retreat (still doing good work today) and appointed George Jepson as Superintendent.

Soon after his introduction into office, after the exercise of some severity towards a violent patient, he passed a sleepless night in anxious cogitations. He felt satisfied that his mode of treatment in this case had tended to irritate rather than control the patient's diseased feelings; and he determined to try the effect of an opposite system... His observations and experience soon led him to abandon the system of terror, and to adopt that which presumed the patient to be generally capable of influence through the kindly affections of the heart; and also in a considerable degree through the medium of the understanding.

It was a practical confirmation of the Quaker belief in "that of God" in everyone.

Some of the Friends who went into prison realised that it was little use to try to save the prisoners' souls while their bodies were so abused by the prison regime. One of the most remarkable of them was Stephen Grellet. He was a French aristocrat whose family lost all their lands in the Revolution and became refugees. He joined Quakers in New York in 1797, after reading William Penn's *No Cross, No Crown*, (which incidentally had been written in prison). He developed a particular interest in visiting gaols. In 1813 he went into Newgate Prison in London, and entered the women's section, against the advice of the staff. It was like a scene in hell. There were nearly three hundred women, as well as babies and children, in two long rooms with scanty dirty straw to sleep on. They were old and young, hardened criminals and pregnant teenagers, some not yet tried or convicted, many seriously ill. They were cooking and eating meagre scraps, while they cursed and fought with one another. Leaving the prison and going to Elizabeth Fry's home nearby, he was in shock: "I described, out of the fullness of my heart, what I had just beheld, stating also that something must be done immediately for those poor suffering children."

Elizabeth Fry reacted in a typically practical way. She bought some flannel, assembled a group of young Quaker women and set them to make baby clothes. She and a friend took these to the prison next day and persuaded the astonished and reluctant Governor to let them visit the women's section. There they dressed every baby and spoke words of comfort to their mothers. Next day they returned with more gifts and enough thick clean straw to make bedding for those who were sick. They spoke to the whole group and prayed with them. June Rose writes: "When Mrs Fry spoke she was transported, serene, confident, infinitely consoling. Her audience listened, as if hypnotised, to her lilting voice with its message of love and hope; as she prayed, there seems no doubt that they too felt momentarily lifted above themselves and relieved of their burdens." Some years later, a woman called Charlotte Newman wrote early on the morning of her execution to thank her, saying, "I have much to be thankful for. I feel much serenity of mind and fortitude. God, of his infinite mercy, grant that I may feel as I do now in the last moments!"

In the next four years, Betsy, as she was known, lived at out of London, had two more babies and lost a four-year-old daughter. She maintained a sporadic interest in prison issues, and started a village school. As soon as she moved back to the city she returned to Newgate with a proposal to open a school for the prisoners' children and juvenile prisoners. "Gently, humbly, but with relentless persistence," says June Rose, "she asked the authorities to at least let her *try* the experiment. It was hard to refuse Mrs Fry." As soon as classes started, taught by a young educated woman who had stolen a watch, the teenage and adult prisoners begged for something similar. This led to the famous occasion when the prison authorities joined Betsy and her ladies' group in a meeting with around seventy prisoners and were astonished at the women's respectful demeanour, modest requests and eagerness to change their lives.

I can't do justice to the range of reforms which were due to Betsy. The details, and the struggles to achieve them, are given in June Rose's biography (see the references below). They included the separation of serious offenders from younger ones whom they might corrupt, and male from female prisoners; the appointment of paid matrons to supervise the women; literacy classes and bible study, with instruction in clothes making, for which the women were paid, so they could build up some funds to help them on release. The Ladies' Association she had set up offered an extra shilling for every five shillings a woman earned. It also provided clothing for those who had none, and even opened a little shop by the gates where the women could buy tea, sugar and haberdashery with their earnings. Betsy campaigned for better material conditions, including a reliable supply of soap.

She proposed a set of rules of conduct, and asked the prisoners to vote yes or no to each of them. Her greatest achievement was to convince the officials involved to see them as fellow human beings. Only ten months after the work started, she was asked to give evidence to a House of Commons committee on London's prisons. This was an unprecedented compliment to a woman, and it brought changes which were supported by government money. It also made her famous.

To our way of thinking her style was autocratic. This was no doubt the cause of her success, since people recognised the clarity of her vision, and found it hard to say no to her! But she was also capable of a wonderful tenderness. At first she was mainly concerned for the prison children, and referred to the adults as "those very wicked women". But her conversations with them and their response to her efforts brought her to see "the individual value of these poor creatures", which she then urged others to recognise. And we should not overlook the personal cost of the work to her. She wrote in her Journal: "My mind has also been deeply affected in attending a poor woman who was executed this morning. I visited her twice; this event has brought me into much feeling by some distressingly nervous sensations in the night... The poor creature murdered her baby; and how inexpressibly awful now to have her life taken away."

Elizabeth Fry brought revolutionary changes working within the constraints of the existing system, its personnel and buildings. But in the United States of America, in the first heady days of independence, there was room for innovation and experiment. Pennsylvania was no longer controlled by the Quakers, but they were still very influential. They founded the world's first penal reform society, the Philadelphia Society for the Relief of Distressed Prisoners, which opened a penitentiary in 1790, whose approach was eventually copied in several hundred prisons worldwide, including the Victorian prisons of Great Britain.

The impulse was religious. The founders recognised that associating together increased the risk of the younger prisoners, more open to reform, being corrupted by the experienced criminals. They also looked at the benefits of silence and contemplation in their own experience of Quaker worship, and wanted to offer these to the convicts. So they were largely housed in single cells; there was solitary confinement for much of the day and silence was enforced when prisoners were together for work and meals. The system was unpleasant enough to meet the public's ideas of retribution and deterrence. But a few voices raised concerns about the effects of segregation and the "rule of silence" on "fragile minds". Stephen Hobhouse experienced this regime as a conscientious objector in the First World War, and in 1922 helped to conduct a public enquiry into the penal system which brought major reforms. He wrote: "It was shown, fairly conclusively, that this aim of retribution, however moral and 'majestic', could not be carried out without doing incalculable harm in most cases both to the prisoner and to the society of which he still remains a part, and often to those who administer his punishment."

The prison experience of conscientious objectors in both world wars breathed new life into the traditional concern with penal matters. We saw how some Quakers expressed their peace testimony by trying to relieve the sufferings caused by war, while others tried to engage with its causes. In a rather similar way, there are Friends today who serve within the system as voluntary prison visitors and chaplains, probation officers and magistrates, and there have been a few prison governors; Duncan Fairn, a Quaker with a strong belief in rehabilitation, was made head of the English Prison Service in 1966. Those in this former group are bound by the Official Secrets Act which prevents them from sharing what they see inside. Meanwhile others feel the system is too inhumane and damaging to continue without radical reform. They often work through non-Quaker organisations like the Prison Reform Trust and the Howard League for Penal Reform, which have always had a strong Quaker membership.

Elizabeth Fry's tradition continues in a variety of ways. The Quaker Canteens in the Northern Ireland prisons during the years of conflict started as a service to prisoners' families, and their staff were later invited into the prisons to do important rehabilitation and reconciliation work with the inmates. Some Friends express their concern about capital punishment by exchanging letters with prisoners on "death row" in US prisons. The Quaker United Nations Office in Geneva has lobbied governments for new international standards in the treatment of women prisoners, and researched the effects of the death penalty on the children of those executed. In my view it is one of the strengths of Quaker testimony that we find Friends using such a range of approaches.

Challenging the morality of punishment

Though she did so much to improve conditions in prison, Elizabeth Fry did not question the need for imprisonment. Only in the twentieth century did Friends begin to ask fundamental questions about the purpose, morality and effectiveness of punishment.

They defined punishing as deliberately causing hurt or deprivation to someone because they have hurt or deprived someone else. In traditional thinking, this infliction of suffering is justified in terms of retribution, rehabilitation, protection of society, and deterrence of others. A fourth claim is that there is no effective alternative. All these justifications have at times been challenged. Friends have been particularly uneasy about retribution because of the biblical injunction, "Render not evil for evil but contrariwise blessing." But they understood that individual citizens have given up their right of revenge to the state ("Don't take the law into your own hands"); and most victims of crime expect the state to get redress for them in this way. Friends have strongly endorsed the importance of rehabilitation and reform; but many of them question whether prison is the best means to achieve it. Incarceration may protect society while the offenders are imprisoned, but this is poor protection if they emerge to offend again. Deterrence is morally questionable too; is it right to hurt one person in the hopes of affecting the actions of someone else?

Prisons are the most institutional form of punishment, but it exists in many spheres of life: parenting, school discipline, workplace sanctions, the armed forces, driving penalties and much besides. Imprisonment is probably the hardest one to change, so it is not surprising that the first sustained Quaker assault on the whole rationale of punishment since John Bellows (as far as I know) came from a Friend working in a different field, the care of difficult children. His name was David Wills.

When I was a schoolchild in the 1940s and 1950s, the corporal punishment of boys was still almost unquestioned, as it had been from time immemorial. Until the mid-nineteenth century all but one of the Quaker schools* beat boys who misbehaved. It is sad that Friends did not make the connection with Elizabeth Fry's telling the House of Commons Committee as early as 1818: "I think I may say we have full power among [the female prisoners], though we use nothing but kindness. I have never proposed a punishment." I was interested to discover that pupil power ended physical punishment at Sidcot School in 1859. The behaviour of harsh teachers led the boys to agree on a strike unanimously. They barricaded themselves in a room with scraps of food until the senior master agreed to negotiate with them. According to the school's official history, "Not one of the teachers ever again laid hands on a scholar."

David Wills started his career in 1922 in a Reform School where staff hit the young people if they annoyed them. In reaction, he trained as a psychiatric social worker, the first in

Britain, as well as joining the Society of Friends. During the war he became Warden of the Barns Hostel in Scotland for disturbed and unbilletable evacuee children. It was here that he forged his philosophy and tried out his ideas with the support of a largely Quaker Board. David believed that punishment (as defined earlier) was unchristian, but he tried to support this view with practical objections to it. He argued that it established a base motive for being good, namely fear. It had been tried all too frequently on the children now in his care and had failed to change their ways. Indeed some of the children actually provoked it as a way of assuaging their guilt feelings about their compulsive behaviour. Other offenders, once they had "paid for their crimes", felt they could "buy" the next ones with an easy conscience. Most crucially, he believed that turning the staff into detectives, police, judges and punishers "...militates against establishment of the relationship which we consider necessary between staff and children—a relationship within which the child must feel himself to be loved."

As an alternative he proposed what is called reparation or restitution. This works well in a small community like a school where there is a common ethos and shared interest in everyone's well-being. Someone who has offended against someone else or the whole community is often feeling guilty, or at least humiliated to be found out. To give her or him a chance to put right the wrong offers a way back into good esteem. They feel they can make up for the hurt they caused, and others will see them as someone who is sorry and has tried to make amends.

I worked for many years in a school for emotionally disturbed teenage boys which dealt with misbehaviour in this way. For instance, if a boy broke a window whether in temper or by accident, he was asked by the community to pick up the fragments, clean out the frame and measure it. He ordered a piece of glass cut to the right size, and did some work to pay for it. When it arrived, he had to putty it in. If he didn't have enough skill an older boy would offer to help him. This is not an easier option than a conventional punishment, and more likely to discourage him from breaking another because it was a logical and practical consequence, and left him with a sense of achievement. In the penal system, community service orders are a first small step in this direction.

When property was stolen or damaged in our school, the culprit was asked to do something extra for the owner, besides paying for a replacement. If someone was seriously hurt, the discussion might need to take into account why the aggressor was driven to do it. Our boys, though labelled as disturbed, showed great insight and compassion in these discussions. In our school, such decisions were made by the whole community of boys and adults in a daily meeting of around fifty people, and the offender was asked if he agreed to the suggestion. David experimented at times with different mechanisms, such as a representative panel of children. The principle, now called "restorative justice" or "restorative practice" was widely adopted in progressive schools, and has been carried forward for many years by the Quaker-led programme *Transforming Conflict*.

It would obviously take a lot of vision, imagination and hard work to create a national justice system based on these principles. Friends took up the challenge in a booklet in 1979 called *Six Quakers look at Crime and Punishment*. David was one of the group. They wrote:

Causing deliberate hurt to another person... not only harms the punished but also degrades those who inflict it, and is a barrier to the working of God's love in us... To do away with punishment is not to abandon safety and control or to move towards disintegration, disorder and lawlessness. A non-punitive approach will not remove the need in some circumstances for restraint or secure containment, but it does mean that restraint and containment should be carried out in a life-enhancing spirit of love and care.

...Reconciliation, restitution and reparation may take longer but... will be more likely to encourage the good in all parties, restore those who are damaged, reduce resentment and bitterness, and enable all those involved to move towards fuller integration.

More recently our Friend Marian Liebmann's definitive book *Restorative Justice* describes how it works in detail in penal and other settings.

Quakers have often supported the idea of rehabilitation, first put forward by John Bellers in 1699. Besides her sewing classes for the women in prison, Elizabeth Fry provided needlework kits and patches of cloth for quilting to the women transported on convict ships to Australia, so they would have something to sell for cash when they landed. In modern times, Friends have pioneered two programmes in which society reaches out to ex-offenders and encourages their attempts to lead a new life. One is the *Alternatives to Violence* (AVP) programme which I mentioned in the chapter on peace. Its premise is that violence is often a reaction to fear or distress which has become habitual and does not deal effectively with the threatening situation. Its exercises are designed to reveal and break the habit of violence and teach new responses. One of the most impressive people I ever met was an American prisoner serving a 120-year sentence. After seven years in gaol during which "I was an animal" (as he told me), he looked at himself and decided he did not want to be like that for the rest of his life. He completed the full AVP programme. It made him realise he needed to catch up on his missed education; so he began to study and then taught other prisoners. He set up the first formal education classes in the prison, begging computers from local businesses when the prison would not supply them, and changed the lives of many other inmates, and even some prison officers, by his love and care for them.

Circles of Support and Accountability were started by Canadian Friends. A small group works with a sex offender on release from prison. They meet him or her every week to assist in the formation of a better life which aims to avoid re-offending. The Circle is supportive but also very challenging. The approach has proved successful, with a much reduced incidence of further offences. It was reported of one focus person in a Circles group that "his own self-punishment, created by these negative feelings and associations, has a far greater impact than any punishment that the state has imposed upon him. After all, his time in prison has come to an end, but his negative feelings that are preventing him from getting on with his life are ongoing." Beyond their specific value in reform, both these programmes symbolise of a community which wants to welcome back those who have harmed it.

The "Six Quakers" later wrote a statement urging Friends to adopt a testimony against punishment. The possibility was discussed at Yearly Meeting 1985, which referred it for consideration by local Meetings across the country. The concern came back to Yearly Meeting two years later. One of the Friends who collated the responses reported, "We found that, although most Friends were willing to abolish public punishment, we were less keen to search our hearts... in the domains where we do have control... We were obliged to report in honesty to Yearly Meeting that Friends were not then united in their attitudes to punishment."

Personal issues

It is when we become parents that we personally face the dilemmas around punishment. My wife and I were lucky in starting our working lives in a school run on the same principles that David Wills used, so we absorbed his thinking. I think I never used any physical punishment on my four children, and I would encourage Quaker parents to avoid it. But I do not want it totally banned, either by Friends or the law, because I think there are worse ways in which people may be cruel to children. Icy disapproval over days may be worse than a quick smack in anger which closes the incident.

But the common law defence of "reasonable chastisement" sometimes protects parents from the legal consequences of actions which would be condemned as assaults if the victims were not their own children. There is force in the "thin end of the wedge" argument, as John Woolman wrote: "Oppression in the extreme appears terrible: but oppression in more refined appearances remains to be oppression; and where the smallest degree of it is cherished it grows stronger and more extensive." However I would be cautious in judging other people's actions when they are trying to do their best in situations in which I am not involved. I think that it is more promising to help them find positive ways to reinforce good behaviour rather than to punish the bad. And I believe that the Quaker way to right action is determined by self-awareness and self-examination, not by writing rules for all to follow.

For further reading

June Rose: *Elizabeth Fry – a biography.* (Quaker Home Service, 1994)

John Lampen: *Mending Hurts* (Swarthmore Lecture, 1987)

Tim Newell: *Forgiving Justice: A Quaker Vision for Criminal Justice* (Swarthmore Lecture, 2000)

Marian Liebmann: *Restorative Justice* (Jessica Kingsley, 2007)

The Arts, Especially Music

Quakers are rightly proud of many heroic episodes in the history of their movement. But one they would probably like to forget is the day, sometime in the 1660s, when the Quaker musician Solomon Eccles made a bonfire of his instruments on Tower Hill in London in obedience, as he said, to "the Voice of the Lord in my heart". When spectators tried to rescue them from the flames, he smashed them with his boots. Eccles was in the fourth generation of a highly talented musical family, and had been very successful himself. His descendants followed his profession rather than his faith; one of his three sons played in the royal orchestras in London and Paris, and his grandson John collaborated with Henry Purcell, wrote some of the tunes of *The Beggar's Opera*, and became Master of the Queen's Music. Ormerod Greenwood lamented in 1978, "Suppose that [Quakers] had loved, understood, [and] fostered music... then we might be talking today about the Eccles family as Germans talk about the family of Bach, who drew their strength... from their Lutheran background."

Previously Friends had not objected to music; Gulielma, who married William Penn, used to play the lute as solace for the blind John Milton. But Friends approved of Solomon's witness, and their rejection of music lasted well into the 20th century. Of all the things which separate us from our Quaker forebears, this testimony against music is hardest to understand. Making music, an activity which seems so innocent in itself, is also encouraged throughout the Bible. And great music, more than any other art, speaks to us in the immediate language of the Spirit.

To understand it we must not think of Bach and Beethoven, but the music which George Fox and his contemporaries knew: drinking songs, love songs, bawdy ballads, recruiting songs, and dances. The restoration of Charles II added the music of the theatre, ostentatious pageants like Purcell's *King Arthur* and the licentious comedies of Congreve. Today we may see no harm in any of these, but they symbolised for Friends the "world" which they must renounce. Even hymns were rejected, because they were at the heart of the church worship which Friends opposed.

Renunciation is so unfashionable today that we may find the teenage Job Scott's agonies on the dance-floor sad, or even funny, but in 1770 they were all too real for him:

> Sometimes when I have stood upon the floor to dance, with a partner by the hand, before all were quite ready, God has arisen in judgement, and smitten me to the very heart... I felt ready to sink under the weight of condemnation and anguish; but resolutely mustering all the stoutness I was master of, I brazened it out till the music called me to the dance, and then I soon drowned the voice of my conviction, became merry and caroused among my companions in dissipation, until time urged a dismission of our jovial assembly and called me to a return, often lonely, to my father's house.

Friends not only disapproved of music and dancing; they were strongly discouraged from going to the theatre or opera, and from reading novels. All these activities were put on a par with hunting and gambling. Because the stories and people in novels are fictitious, how could they be consistent with the Quaker testimony to truth? Friends could not see how a fiction could tell the truth about social conditions or the human heart; and even if it could, surely truth spoken in plain words must be better. Amelia Opie gave up writing novels when she joined the Society of Friends in 1825 under the influence of Elizabeth Fry and her family. It was a pity, since her *Adeline Mowbray* had explored women's education, marriage ethics, and the abolition of slavery, all themes which were important to Friends.

Fortunately reading and even writing poetry was allowed, so

she continued to write in verse. Thomas Ellwood, who used to read to Milton and was a friend of William Penn, had written poems; and Job Scott in the late eighteenth century included some of his poems in his journal. John Greenleaf Whittier (1807–1892) was one of the most highly regarded American poets of his day, and his lines beginning "Dear Lord and Father of mankind" are still a favourite hymn. He used poems to urge the abolition of slavery. But Quakers only approved poetry if it had a firm moral tone. Elizabeth Fry's sister Priscilla published a book called *Gurney's Select Hymns* in 1818, which ran into ten editions by 1848. Sadly it was not for singing, but only for memorising and meditation.

Drawing attracted less disapproval, possibly because of the valuable labours and artistry of the Quaker botanists. The vanity associated with oil portraits was unacceptable for a long time, though from the start of the nineteenth century, Quaker journals and memoirs* often included an engraved portrait of their subject. But as late as 1847 there were letters in Quaker periodicals objecting to this practice.

Caroline Graveson wrote in 1937: "The highest culture carries restraint, and the very cuttings off practiced by Friends of the older day, their ordered houses and dress and pursuits, gave to their lives some quality of art which our own more inclusive existences often seem to miss." Friends did create two art forms of their own, which beautifully expressed their particular values. One was the Quaker Meeting House, whose bare simplicity and fine proportions matched the spirit of their worship, a gentle rebuke to more fashionable types of religious architecture. The other was the Quaker journal, or account of a life, which searched for the right language to express the inexpressible, and tells stories of insights, encounters, dreams and mysterious guidance which were until recently part of our shared heritage. Here is a passage from the Journal of Thomas Ellwood, telling how he occupied himself in prison, never having worked at a trade, to show the quality of some of that writing:

And now the chief thing I wanted was employment, which scarce any wanted but myself, for the rest of the company were generally tradesmen... Of these divers were tailors, some masters, some journeymen; and with these I most inclined to settle. But because I was too much of a novice to be entrusted with their work, lest I should spoil the garment, I got work from a hosier in Cheapside, which was to make night waistcoats of red and yellow flannel for women and children. And with this, I entered myself among the tailors, and so spent those leisure hours with innocency and pleasure, which want of business would have made tedious.

The ban on music

The ban on music originally arose from the high value they put on it: "very sweet and refreshing," wrotes Robert Barclay in 1675, "when it proceeds from a true sense of God's love in the heart and arises from the divine influence of the Spirit, which leads souls to breathe forth either a sweet harmony or words suitable to the present condition." George Fox sang hymns to wear out a fiddler sent into his dungeon to drown his voice; but he objected to singing psalms as advised by a priest to whom he went for counsel, because the words did not express his state of mind. He was always angered by formality and insincerity in religious worship, and this was typified by singing a hymn or psalm, regardless of what it said, just because this was the fourteenth morning of the month, or because it had been chosen by the parson. "Such singing," said Barclay, "doth more please the carnal ears of men that the pure ears of the Lord, who abhors all lying and hypocrisy " Music, he says, can belong to God, but it also has a dangerous and seductive charm.

As so often in religion, the struggles and insights of one generation became the unthinking dogma of the next. Thomas

Clarkson (not a Friend) undertook to justify Quaker attitudes to music in his *Portraiture of Quakerism* of 1806. He said Friends realise that instrumental music is innocent in itself, though vocal music (as I mentioned before) was often contaminated by the character of its words. But Quakers were concerned that the amount of skill and practice required for acceptable performance reduced the time for spiritual contemplation. Skill aroused vanity, especially among the unmarried girls who were the usual performers. Society saw music as a useful accomplishment in finding a life partner which was often dropped after marriage. (No married woman plays music in any of Jane Austen's novels.) Fundamentally music was a sensual pleasure, and Clarkson wrote, "The Quakers believe that all sensual desires should be… discouraged as much as possible, as being opposed to those spiritual feelings which constitute the only perfect enjoyment of a Christian."

And paradoxically it is at this point, where I disagree with them most strongly, that I begin to understand those Friends' position. I worry about the effect on children of violent scenes on television, or computer games of exterminating the "baddies", with their dubious moral influence and their addictive qualities. I am concerned about today's flood of trivial and misleading information which occupies my mind and distracts it from things of more spiritual benefit to me; and the devices which deliver it wherever we are, cutting us off from mindfulness in the present place and moment. Surely our testimony to simplicity is not only about external objects and the physical environment, but also about how we order our inner space. So I feel some affinity with the earlier Quaker view that a line must be drawn somewhere. I am sure that they drew it in the wrong place and excluded too much that is of value. But I think I should examine my own use of time rather than dismiss them as killjoys and bigots.

That is not to approve of what they did. A Friend was disowned by the Society in 1804 because "she encourages and approves her children being taught the practice of music". James Backhouse issued a pamphlet against the York Musical Festival of 1825 in which he exhorted all Christians who were inclined to attend it to "put away the evil of their doings from before the Lord's eyes." An article in the *British Friend* in 1857 advises its readers that "in Germany and Paris, amongst a hundred sufferers of a certain class of residents in the lunatic asylum, you will find a fourth who are or were musicians."

Such pronouncements provoked a reaction, and their extreme tone suggests that the writers were already fighting a losing battle. The "gay" or worldly Friends of Elizabeth Fry's youth thought it no harm to enjoy music. Her husband loved the opera. One Quaker who played the flute became a "plain" Friend later; so he took his flute once a year to the top of the Monument in London and played it where he hoped it would do no harm!

Social attitudes to music changed drastically in the age of Beethoven; the role of music as a diversion diminished, and it acquired a new status as a type of spiritual biography. The drawing room and dance floor gave place to the concert hall. Beethoven himself is quoted as saying: "Music is a higher revelation than all wisdom and philosophy. Music is the electrical soil in which the spirit lives, thinks and invents." Did the Quakers of the time not see that music can nourish our spiritual lives? Were they deaf to its power to sympathise and console in hard times, to encourage and inspire? Not all of them; Elizabeth Fry wrote of her "regret that we as a Society so wholly give up delighting the ear by sound. Surely He who formed the ear and the heart would not have given these tastes and powers without some purpose for them." But officially the argument was noted only to be refuted. The following passage from a London Yearly Meeting Epistle was thought so apt that it reappeared in the 1860 edition of Ireland Yearly Meeting's Book of Discipline, still current in the early years of the twentieth century:

That which is of the character ordinarily designated as sacred music not unfrequently stimulates expressions and feelings which are far from being the genuine breathings of a renewed heart, and tends to produce an excitement often unhappily mistaken for devotion, and to withdraw the soul from that quiet humble and retired frame in which prayer and praise may truly be offered with the spirit and with the understanding also... That music on the other hand which does not in any degree partake of the character usually designated as sacred has, we fear, in innumerable instances allured the feet of the young to the lightness, the gaiety and even the dissipation of the world, and thus proved among the many snares against which we are enjoined fervently to pray, "Lead us not into temptation".

The general change in attitudes to music was assisted by the mass production of pianos and printed music. More of the community came to know and love serious music, as novels like *Middlemarch* show. Another influence was the evangelical revival, which had a powerful effect on our Society, particularly in Ireland. Though Friends' Meetings would not sing hymns in their worship, they recognised how effective they were in gaining and keeping converts in other denominations. Slowly Quaker attitudes began to change in line with the spirit of the times.

The nineteenth century also recognised the value of music in education. In 1878, the Friends' School at Lisburn near Belfast (where no music was allowed) was inundated with requests from parents. The Quarterly Meeting which regulated the school "became a battlefield", but after two years a piano was agreed so long as it was not bought with school money. For years all accounts relating to music were kept strictly separate from school accounts! Sidcot School was given its first piano to retain a senior girl "of specially good influence" (not a Quaker) who was leaving because there was no music instruction; but both the School Committee and the General Meeting were so evenly divided that the difficulty was resolved by a neighbouring Friend making her drawing-room available for lessons. Leighton Park, founded a few years later, escaped such difficulties. A music teacher was soon appointed, and its 1902 prospectus proudly announces that instrumental and vocal music is encouraged, even at "school socials". In the same year Sidcot started an annual concert in the local village in aid of a charitable cause.

It took Friends even longer to give up the idea that art, to be valuable, must be edifying. Caroline Graveson in her Swarthmore Lecture *Religion and Culture* takes a backward look at "our Quaker forefathers' fear of culture". Even in 1937 she needed to remind Friends that "God is the God of Beauty and Truth as well as Goodness", and to suggest that we were still rather one-sided in our practice of the Quaker doctrine that all life is sacramental. "...The sheer stuff of things which by the inspiration of God blowing through the minds of men have become great literature and music and art, have we drawn these sufficiently into the sacramental life?" She even challenged the Quaker notion* that art must be elevated and sublime to be worthy of our attention: "God is in all fitness of sound and measure, whether the result be Bach's Passion Music or a nursery jingle. The quantity of God, so to speak, varies in the different examples, but His quality of beauty in fitness remains the same."

But only in Ormerod Greenwood's Swarthmore Lecture in 1978 do we find a full-blooded Quaker defence of art as essential to our souls' health, even when it is trivial, amoral or anarchic. From the same Yearly Meeting sprang an organisation called The Leaveners to run programmes of arts-based workshops and events that drew on Quaker values to explore issues relating to human rights, social justice, peace and spirituality through participatory drama, music and visual arts activities. Among these were the oratorios *The Gates of Greenhorn* and *The Cry of the Earth* which were performed to large audiences in London and

45

Birmingham.

Why did it take so long for this change to come? We can partly blame Quaker conservatism and the dead hand of tradition, as the stories of the school pianos show. But for a deeper understanding we must go back to Solomon Eccles, the Friend with whom it all started. Fortunately we have his own account of what led him to make his bonfire of instruments on Tower Hill. *A Musick-Lector* is unusual among Quaker writing of the time in being a genuine dialogue between different points of view: there is an Anglican musician who thinks music is a gift of God, a Baptist who affirms it to be an innocent pastime, and a Quaker (Eccles himself) who "being formerly of that Art, doth give his Judgment and Sentence against it; but yet approves of the Musick that pleaseth God". The Quaker, of course, wins in the end. We might not agree with his arguments, based largely on selected Bible texts; but they are rational and not fanatical. His phrase "the Musick which pleaseth God" recalls a passage in which George Fox describes the start of his own mission: "I was to bring [people] off from all the world's fellowships, and prayings, and singings, which stood in forms without power... that they might pray in the Holy Ghost, and sing in the spirit and with the grace that comes by Jesus, making melody in their hearts to the Lord..."

Eccles decided that the Lord's music was a silent music of the soul. But it is clear that it was an enormous sacrifice to give up the art which he loved. The consequences were not just financial and professional, but went to the core of his being. The moment of truth came when he was playing in a quintet, "and the parts hit with the Fuige, and came in with the Discords and Concords so very lovely" and someone expressed his pleasure using an oath. Eccles was immediately convinced he was being asked to put it all behind him. Ormerod Greenwood again:

At one of those moments which occur rarely in a musician's

or anyone else's lifetime, when everything is going perfectly and you are lifted out of this world in to another dimension and the only thing you can feel is unspeakable content and harmony which you wish might never cease—at this very moment Solomon Eccles tears himself away from the experience of Transfiguration... because he feels that it is "so very lovely, that it took very much with that part which stands not in unity with the Lord".

For further reading

Ormerod Greenwood: *Signs of Life* (Swarthmore Lecture, 1978)

Brenda Clifft Heales and Chris Cook: *Images and Silence* (Swarthmore Lecture, 1992)

A Musick Lector is available online at www.qhpress.org/texts/eccles.html

Experience, Belief and Theology

The humble, meek, merciful, just, pious, and devout souls are everywhere of one religion; and when death has taken off the mask they will know one another, though the divers liveries they wear here makes them strangers. This world is a form; our bodies are forms; and no visible acts of devotion can be without forms. But yet the less form in religion the better, since God is a Spirit; for the more mental our worship, the more adequate to the nature of God; the more silent, the more suitable to the language of a Spirit. *William Penn (1693)*

There is a principle which is pure, placed in the human mind, which in different places and ages hath different names; it is, however, pure and proceeds from God. It is deep and inward, confined to no forms of religion nor excluded from any where the heart stands in perfect sincerity. In whomsoever this takes root and grows, of what nation soever, they become brethren. *John Woolman, (1762)*

These two statements from our past go to the heart of the Quaker experience. They explain how a group of Quakers may worship comfortably together even if one is a traditional Christian, another is a lapsed church member, another a Buddhist, another a seeker looking around for some certainty; there may be those present who do not believe in a personal God or prefer not to use the word God at all. Two Bosnian Muslims who attended my local meeting for worship said afterwards, "You say God and we say Allah, but at the level of the spirit we are one." William Penn and John Woolman believed there is, or at least can be, a common experience uniting the worshipping group.

George Fox said of himself at the start of his mission, "I was to bring people off from Jewish [i.e. Old Testament] ceremonies

48

and from heathenish fables and from men's inventions and windy doctrines, by which they blowed the people about this way and the other way, from sect to sect." His opposition to priests and ministers arose from his belief that "Christ has come to teach his people himself". He believed this so passionately that he has shocked some modern Quakers by the language he used and the way he interrupted church sermons and berated what he called "professors", that is, those who professed a faith they did not live.

Edward Grubb wrote of Fox's first followers, "Some of them were men and women of little learning; others, on the contrary, were already preachers, and versed in the theology of the day. But they all agreed with Fox that Christianity was not a scheme of doctrine to be believed, but an experience to be entered into, and a life to be lived; and they tended, therefore, to regard theology as a collection of 'notions' of no importance, and possibly even a hindrance, to the religious life."

But they could not avoid using such notions themselves. When they preached they needed an understandable language which their audience shared, and in that time and place this was bound to be Christian terminology. In consequence they got into continual trouble for how they reinterpreted it. James Nayler was attacked in court in 1652, "Didst thou not write a paper, wherein was mentioned that if thou thinkest to be saved by that Christ which died at Jerusalem thou art deceived?" He gave the memorable answer, "If I cannot witness Christ nearer than Jerusalem, I shall have no benefit by him; but I own no other Christ but that who witnessed a good confession before Pontius Pilate; which Christ I witness suffering in me now." Like his fellow Quakers he identified his inner voice as "the inward Christ"; the revelations he received demonstrated Jesus' promise to come again to his people.

Penn, an enthusiastic youngster recently convinced of the truth of Quakerism, wrote a pamphlet in 1668 called *The Sandy*

Foundation Shaken (he was good at inventing titles). He challenged the "generally believed and applauded doctrines of one God subsisting in three distinct and separate persons", though he did not state his own beliefs clearly. The book was attacked as "a horrid and abominable piece against the Holy Trinity", and Penn found himself imprisoned in the Tower of London for blasphemy. There he penned a sequel setting out his own beliefs, *Innocency with her Open Face*, with copious quotations from scripture to support them. This and his next book, *No Cross, No Crown*, were enough to get his release eventually, though the fact that his father was an Admiral probably helped. When George Fox's Journal was prepared for publication twenty-five years later, Penn tried to express the essence of the Quaker message: to witness to "the principle of God in man", why it was there, how they might distinguish it from their mundane thinking, and what it could do for them.

It is remarkable that, though Quakers were quick to condemn what they saw as false religion and theology, they did not seek to replace it with dogmas of their own, but gave primacy to what each person discerned in her or his own heart. Human nature being what it is, they had to modify this position when the actions of some Friends claiming divine inspiration brought the whole group into danger. But the test they then adopted was that individuals should bring their "leadings" to a group of Quakers in worship, who would discern whether these came from God, and the person would abide by the meeting's conclusion. Quakers are still encouraged to use this test today.

"The word of God (whether of exhortation or instruction)," wrote Isaac Penington, "is a gift which is to be waited for..." I hope that most modern Friends, whether they use god-language or not, accept that we can receive such guidance if we wait for it. We can do this from moment to moment; we don't have to wait for our next Quaker meeting. Guidance generally takes one of four forms:

(i) An insight into oneself, revealing what is wrong in one's life and showing the way to change.

(ii) An insight into the state of the world or some particular issue which needs to be addressed.

(iii) What action to take in a decision one knows one must make.

(iv) An unexpected call to action.

As an example of (i) we can take George Fox's advice to Oliver Cromwell's daughter when she was depressed:

"What the Light [of God] doth make manifest and discover— temptations, confusions, distractions, distempers—do not look at the temptations, confusions, corruptions, but at the Light that... makes them manifest; and with the same Light you will... receive power to stand against them."

(ii) was shown in the illumination of a single Friend in her meeting which eventually led to the Quaker campaign against the use of child soldiers mentioned in chapter 2. (iii) is common in Quaker experience, in small things as well as large. If I am in a difficult conversation, I try to surrender my own point of view, calm myself and allow a greater wisdom to guide me. And when my wife and I were considering whether to take our family to live in Ulster during the years of violence, we took the question to meeting for worship for several weeks until each of us separately felt clear what to do.

(ii) and (iii) together show the normal path by which a Quaker concern develops into action. It may take many years; Quaker witness against slavery began with a declaration by one Meeting near Philadelphia in 1688, and did not produce tangible results outside the Quaker community till the early nineteenth century.

(iv) is the most mysterious category. There is a classic story of Thomas Waring, a Quaker who received an inexplicable prompting to take horse late at night and ride to Ross-on-Wye. There he saw one lighted window and felt sure that it was the place he must visit. He was just in time to save a desperate young woman from killing herself. The story has the feel of a Quaker myth, yet one of my closest friends has twice received similar inward messages which led to her preventing two suicides. However much we may rationalize and explain our Quaker experience, our descriptions remain "notions" which cannot account for everything.

Changes of emphasis

The belief that we should utterly rely on guidance was strong in the eighteenth century, the so-called Quietist period. It can be illustrated from a passage in the American Job Scott's Journal describing a message which came to him as he prepared to speak in meeting:

> I saw there were many subjects on which a man might either muse or speak... but alas! we cannot choose aright for ourselves, any more than we know what to pray for, without [divine] assistance ... This pertinent lesson was opened to my mind: "Trust in the Lord and lean not to thine own satisfaction... Only be thou still and wait my time and my word of life and command, and I will open and none shall shut. But when I shut, neither thou nor any else can ever open."

Such total reliance on inspiration had its dangers. Quakers became obsessed with their life as a secluded and conforming community. Meetings for worship lasted one and a half to two hours, with little or no spoken ministry*, and quite young children were expected to attend with no instruction in what it was all about. When there was ministry, it seldom took the form of a call to social action; if it did, some influential Friend was likely to say that "The time for that has not yet come." Friends became shy of mingling with society because they mistrusted its values and beliefs; the peculiar Quaker dress and speech customs reinforced this seclusion. Friends were told to avoid intellectual stimulus, and that regular systematic teaching of scriptural doctrine was incompatible with Quakerism. Couples wanting to marry had to come to a Meeting for Clearness which decided if they could wed; and the membership* of any Friend marrying a non-Quaker was terminated.

Inevitably there was a reaction, but it came slowly. When some Friends became rich from their banking, trading and manufacturing activities, it caused problems for a religious Society devoted to plainness and simplicity. Their solution was to give away large amounts of money. To do so effectively they had to engage with the world and this exposed them to other people's thinking. The concerns which arose over slavery and prisons could only be pursued in co-operation with non-Quakers. In 1833, after a change in the law, Joseph Sturge became the first Quaker Member of Parliament, followed by the prominent and influential John Bright. William Allen, Stephen Grellet and Elizabeth Fry all canvassed their ideas with government figures and even royalty in Britain and across Europe.

Quaker religious ideas were changing too under the influence of the religious revival associated with John Wesley, which brought a renewed respect for the words of scripture. Many Friends were attracted by this and compared the energy of the new evangelical churches with their own sleepiness. It roused an interest in Quaker missionary work in Britain and overseas, which required printed materials to set forth the Quaker faith. In 1803 Quakers appeared at the inauguration of the British and Foreign Bible Society, to the astonishment of the other representatives. The evangelical tendency took hold,and by the 1850s many Quakers were putting their primary faith in the bible and the Christian doctrine of salvation, and mistrusting the practice of waiting on God for inspiration. In the United States the contrasting viewpoints actually split Quakers into two groups, one of which resembled other nonconformist churches, while the other stayed with the British tradition of largely silent and unprogrammed worship.

In Britain involvement in public affairs caused great anxiety for many years, and even Yearly Meeting Epistles* warned against them, urging that Friends should be "quiet in the land". Every change, from altering the inscriptions and dimensions of gravestones to founding Adult Schools for the poor, became controversial. Modern Friends enjoy taking credit for the anti-slavery campaign, and the work of Elizabeth Fry and other reformers, but at the time a majority of the Society probably disapproved of them. The conservatives were distressed to see Friends starting to abandon the plain style of dress and language which had marked them off from everyone else.

The move from seclusion and waiting on God in silence to a committed engagement with public issues, however reluctant, drew on gospel inspiration and was a crucial step on the path to modern Quakerism. It led to social concerns for which Friends are still respected and valued, as well as vigorous missionary activity in India, Ceylon, China, Syria, Madagascar and elsewhere. In 1846 Britain Yearly Meeting could agree to provide relief in Ireland during the potato famine. In the next half-century the Quaker chocolate makers demonstrated and proclaimed the duty of employers to meet the physical and social needs of their workforce through housing provision, social amenities and decent working conditions.

1850-1900 was a period of striking Quaker social witness. But it also marked a low point in the spiritual life of Britain Yearly Meeting and a marked decline in membership. The control exercised by older members, born into Quaker families, was a continual obstacle to change. There were not many memorable writers on spiritual matters. An exception was Caroline Stephen, unusual among Victorian Friends in being a convert, not a birthright Quaker. She was the daughter of James Stephen, the Undersecretary of State who implemented the Anti-slavery Act, and aunt of Virginia Woolf. She believed that the root of Quakerism was a mystical attitude to religious questions, and wrote: "Within the last century there has been a very marked recoil in the Society at large from what was felt to be too exclusive a reliance on the doctrine of the Inner Light. There are however at the present time indications of a tendency, specially among the young, to revert to the ancient and more specially Quaker view".

In 1895 Yearly Meeting at last faced these tensions by holding a conference in Manchester to consider the state of the Society. The 27-year old John Wilhelm Rowntree, terminally ill and almost blind, led the impetus for change. Neave Brayshaw wrote that "He saw that the Society of Friends had a message to give that was not elsewhere being given, able to reach many who were not otherwise being reached, and he made earnest appeal for the spiritual and intellectual equipment of its members that would enable them to give forth the message with power." Two consequences of this plea were the establishment of Woodbrooke College in Birmingham in 1903 as a Quaker study and training centre; and the writing of a six-volume history of Quakers, meticulously researched, which inspired Friends by describing the vision and energy of the first Friends. Rufus Jones, an American scholar who participated in both developments, followed Caroline Stephen in placing the origins of Quakerism firmly in the mystical tradition which was (in Woolman's words) "confined to no forms of religion nor excluded from any where the heart stands in perfect sincerity".

Participants at the Conference were encouraged to accept the findings of bible scholarship and not consider the entire book infallible. Modern thought was not evil but largely a blessing. Friends should in honesty accept the main principles of evolution, and not believe in the inevitable depravity of the human soul. They were urged to oppose all social conditions which reduced freedom and prevented the true development of character, and to think for themselves, trusting in the inspiration of the Spirit to reveal the truth. It is hard for us today to imagine what a transformation this was for the many Friends who had been taught to take a reactionary position on such issues or to avoid them entirely.

Caroline Stephen approved, saying: "The voluntary exclusion of disturbing influences is a very dangerous resource... Experience... does conclusively prove, to ourselves at any rate, that disturbance by the thoughts of others is one of the most fertilising and purifying processes to which our own thought can be subjected". That conference was the turning point which established modern Quakerism, still based in Christianity but no longer dogmatic; not cut off from the world around it but proud of its traditions of service, opposition to war and worship; and free as it had been at its beginnings to analyse and express its peculiar theology.

A new transition?

In the last twenty years or more there are signs that we are in a new period of transition. There has been much controversial Quaker writing asking what is essentially Quaker. Much of it centres on belief in God and our Christian heritage, asking whether these are essential truths or just vestiges of the beliefs of earlier times. Whenever I ask Quakers what they believe, I find their views lie at every point along a spectrum which does not easily divide into clear groupings. So I think it is a pity that some Friends write as if there were polarised positions (universalist/Christian, nontheist/theist).

The ideas currently being debated would probably be described by early Friends as "notions", unnecessary attempts to fit spiritual realities into conceptual frameworks. This is reflected in the refusal throughout our history to adopt a creed. But in spite of the Quaker mistrust of creeds, we do need a language to understand and conceptualise our experiences. It is difficult to identify or remember them if we cannot put them into words. I believe that the experiences Quakers call guidance* are very common, but most people today do not have a terminology with which to explore them.

There is a tension between our encounters with the Light and the way we try to describe them. Until a point in the mid-twentieth century, Friends were comfortable with god-language, though they did not accept everything said in it; so there was a shared understanding of what underpinned Quaker worship and our business method which was often described as "seeking the will of God" in the matter under discussion. Then the character of the Society changed as many people came into it who did not accept this language. Some were attracted by our peace witness and had little interest in "religion"; others were looking for a refuge from whatever form Christianity had taken in the church of their youth. Most recently, changes in the ways religion is taught in school mean that the writings of early Friends, and even much of the bible, barely make sense to many young readers. Since Quakers traditionally do not proselytise and give little religious teaching in their meetings, many of us lack tools to describe our spiritual lives in words which others can understand.

But although we no longer have a shared language we can recognise that we do have common experiences. Many Friends from the earliest days till now have witnessed that they were led by something beyond their conscious planning mind, and guided to do things they would never have expected or planned. Some experience this "something" as a personal guide, others as an impersonal force. These experiences, as William James says in *The Varieties of Religious Experience*, are authentic and I do not think anyone should cast doubt on them. But when we ask, "Where do they come from?" we enter the realm of "notions".

People have found different ways to name and explain their source, from self-delusion or telepathy to "the Buddha-mind" and "the collective unconscious", and from these to the angels and dreams of the bible and "the Inward Teacher" whom Quakers in the past invoked. Since there is no way to prove which (if any) of the explanations is correct, people generally choose one which is based on their previous assumptions. As a result their debates often generate more heat than light. No less an authority than Carl Jung said that the question whether the experience of the Spirit comes from within us or from a power outside us is meaningless; his answer was "both". We would do well to take to heart William Penn's words about worship, "The more silent, the more suitable to the language of a Spirit."

I want to finish by saying something about guidance as I have known it. This is described in most of the old Quaker Journals; and I and many of my Quaker friends have found that our experiences are essentially the same, though our descriptive language may be different. Personal guidance has occasionally come to me out of the blue, particularly during a difficult situation. For example I may suddenly know the right thing to say to a distressed person, different from what I would have planned. But more often I have needed time to empty my mind of its own preferences and fears, and, as George Fox urged, "wait in the Light" until clearness comes—which does not happen every time. The message is usually unexpected and sometimes frightening; and I take these as signs that it comes from something beyond my conscious mind. As I said earlier the question of whether it is from my deepest self or an outside source does not seem important or helpful to me.

When I am aware of something calling for my attention, and I don't see clearly at first what it is, my response is to wait in the Light. As I make myself still the issue becomes clearer. It may be something wrong in myself, or an outside problem which concerns me. That is followed by a strong sense of the need for change or action. (Such was the experience of the Friend who initiated the concern to help child soldiers.) It may be followed by the conviction of something which I myself should do. The action is often only a first step, and it's usually unclear what the outcome will be. In 1998 I felt a strong call to return to Uganda, ten years after my previous two visits. I could not have said why. And I certainly could not have foreseen the work in landmine issues, peace-building, community development, nursery education and adult literacy which flowed from obeying it.

The waiting can take several days, possibly much longer. There is frequently a sense of turmoil until a decision is made. In 1659 Thomas Elwood wrote, "The general trouble and confusion of mind which had for some days laid heavy upon me and pressed me down... began now to wear off; and some glimmerings of light began to break forth in me". When I have committed myself, I have found that the confusion is replaced by a sense of rightness and peace, even though I may not yet see how to proceed. This calm after the storm tells me that I have discerned correctly. And frequently I have had a second confirmation in the form of assistance which I had not foreseen: an unexpected ally, or the opening of a new door to action. When my wife and I committed ourselves to move with our family to Northern Ireland, we had no idea how we would live; but not long afterwards we were surprised to be offered financial support. Quakers have different ways of explaining such experiences; but the Quaker phrase "when way opens" points to the fact that they frequently occur.

I should make it clear that in larger issues the discernment* process often does not produce a full and clear plan of action. The Quakers of Job Scott's day expected to be led by God every step of the way. In my own experience, once I have accepted the call, there is plenty of work for my intelligence to do, and great need of advice and support from others. However Quakers are rather suspicious of modern management practice with its aims, objectives and indicators of success. If I am doing what I would call God's work, I need to trust that I am "in good hands" and to respond sensitively and flexibly to what unfolds. John Woolman wrote "I have gone forward, not as one travelling in a road cast up and well-prepared, but as a man walking through a miry place, in which are stones here and there, safe to step on; but so situated that one step being taken, time is necessary to see where to step next." This describes how my nineteen years' work in Uganda took shape.

What I have said about my personal experience applies to group discernment too, with the added need of sensitivity to one another. The Quaker business meeting is in essence a meeting for worship, and we expect it to come to unity in its decisions. Yearly Meeting has recommended its members to "work with one another in a humble and loving spirit, each giving to others credit for purity of motive, notwithstanding differences of opinion, and being ready to accept the decision of the meeting even when it may not accord with his own judgement." In 1982 a group of Yearly Meeting employees asked their employers to divert the part of their income tax attributable to military purposes to non-military uses. I spoke to some members of the committee which employed them beforehand and sensed a strong feeling against breaking the law in this way and imperilling our charitable status. Yet when they met in worship to consider the question, they felt unmistakably guided to do so. Their discernment was later endorsed by the Yearly Meeting in session.

I can hesitate between trust and scepticism on a multitude of issues, such as the existence of God and immortality. But my belief in guidance has scarcely wavered, and it is that which keeps me a Quaker.

A Glossary of Terms used by Quakers in a Particular Sense

Based on *Quakerspeak* by Alastair Heron (2008)

Area Meeting: Formerly called Monthly Meetings, Area Meetings consist of a group of Local Meetings within a geographical area. Most members of the Society are recorded by minute as belonging to an Area Meeting and are attached to one of its Local Meetings.

Attender: Someone who comes regularly to worship at a Quaker Meeting who is not in membership.

Concern: The special Quaker use of this term is to denote a divine imperative to action laid inwardly on a person or group. Such awareness needs to be tested in a religiously valid way, most often by bringing it to the Local or Area Meeting to search together in worship to see whether this is actually what God wants.

Discernment: Not a specifically Quaker term, but found generally in writings on the spiritual life, referring to the process of perceiving the will of God through close attention to the promptings of the Spirit. It is therefore important for Quakers in their individual lives and in corporate decision making.

Epistles: A letter issued by a Yearly Meeting or other gathering in session, and agreed to by everyone present. It is not addressed to an individual, but to a group (usually Quaker) and often nowadays "to Friends everywhere".

Guidance: Quakers often use this word to denote an inner prompting to recognise some need, task or stance and then to carry it through. Being guided often means giving up our own ideas and wishes; it has been described by Friends as being led by the Light or the Spirit, or obeying God's will instead of our own.

Leadings: A Quaker term for what many would refer to as "inner guidance". Friends believed that true leadings come from God, and that we must learn to distinguish them from the prompts of our own desires, prudence or expedience. A leading may lead to a concern, usually tested by Quakers looking for discernment together in worship.

Journals and **Memoirs:** A Quaker Journal is not a diary in the usual sense but a record of the writer's "experience of the goodness of God" (Woolman). If a prominent Friend did not leave a Journal, his or her meeting might assemble a Memoir using passages from letters and other writings, with the same intention.

Local Meeting: Previously called Preparative Meetings or Recognised Meetings, these are the groups of Friends who worship together regularly. In most cases a Local Meeting is centred on a Meeting House.

Meeting for Worship: The silence-based Quaker equivalent of a church service. Originally lasting several hours, the practice has slowly evolved to the present point at which it is expected to last about one hour.

Member: Membership of the Religious Society of Friends is normally acquired by application to an Area Meeting. Those applying are visited by two Friends appointed by the Area Meeting, to ensure that the applicant is sufficiently familiar with the heritage and testimonies of Quakers and in unity with its views and practices. The practice of Members registering their children at birth as Quakers has ended.

Ministry: Any kind of service in which the gifts of a Friend are matched to the needs of the Society of Friends or the world. "Spoken" or "vocal ministry" refers to what an individual speaks during a meeting for worship. Until recently it was understood that the call to offer spoken ministry should arise from a clear sense that it came from the Holy Spirit.

Notion: Quakers speak of Christianity not being a "notion" but "a Way." Notion is a negative term for a concept which is a creation of the mind. The intellect engages with it and gives it importance, but it is only a provisional explanation of our experience which certainly does not tell the whole truth about it and may well be wholly mistaken. Quakers felt that the Christian creeds were composed largely of notions.

Quaker schools: Private schools founded by Quakers in the nineteenth century to provide education with a Quaker ethos to children of Friends and attenders. They are each governed by a largely Quaker Board. They continue but only a minority of staff and pupils are now Quakers. Some Friends today are uncomfortable about there being fee-paying schools under Quaker auspices.

Quaker United Nations Offices (QUNO): These are located in Geneva and New York, and have Observer Status at the UN. Through research, dialogue and lobbying, they can play an active part in influencing UN resolutions and programmes. They also provide many opportunities for diplomats to meet informally in quiet acceptable neutral surroundings for confidential conversations.

Swarthmore Lecture: A lecture delivered annually when Yearly Meeting gathers, but not forming part of the proceedings. It is usual for a full version to be published simultaneously. It serves to bring before the public the spirit, aims and fundamental principles of Friends and to interpret further to members of the Society their message and mission. The first lecture was delivered in 1908.

Testimony: The totality of Quaker thought and action on a particular concern, arising from the interplay of worship, research and practical action. Testimonies are continually evolving in the light of experience and as new insights arise. They sometimes lapse when the need has passed or the context changed (for instance the testimony to "plain dress"), but are not formally ended.

Yearly Meeting: "Britain Yearly Meeting" denotes both the final constitutional body of the Religious Society of Friends (Quakers) in Britain, and the annual gathering of those in membership, all of whom have the right to take part in its procedures. In most countries where there are Quakers there is a single Yearly Meeting, which may be very small. In the USA and Kenya however there are many Yearly Meetings in the country.

CHRISTIAN
ALTERNATIVE

Christian Alternative

THE NEW OPEN SPACES

Throughout the two thousand years of Christian tradition there have been, and still are, groups and individuals that exist in the margins and upon the edge of faith. But in Christianity's contrapuntal history it has often been these outcasts and pioneers that have forged contemporary orthodoxy out of former radicalism as belief evolves to engage with and encompass the ever-changing social and scientific realities. Real faith lies not in the comfortable certainties of the Orthodox, but somewhere in a half-glimpsed hinterland on the dirt track to Emmaus, where the Death of God meets the Resurrection, where the supernatural Christ meets the historical Jesus, and where the revolution liberates both the oppressed and the oppressors.

Welcome to Christian Alternative... a space at the edge where the light shines through.
If you have enjoyed this book, why not tell other readers by posting a review on your preferred book site.

Recent bestsellers from Christian Alternative are:

Bread Not Stones
The Autobiography of An Eventful Life
Una Kroll
The spiritual autobiography of a truly remarkable woman
and a history of the struggle for ordination in the Church of
England.
Paperback: 978-1-78279-804-0 ebook: 978-1-78279-805-7

The Quaker Way
A Rediscovery
Rex Ambler
Although fairly well known, Quakerism is not well understood.
The purpose of this book is to explain how Quakerism works as
a spiritual practice.
Paperback: 978-1-78099-657-8 ebook: 978-1-78099-658-5

Blue Sky God
The Evolution of Science and Christianity
Don MacGregor
Quantum consciousness, morphic fields and blue-sky
thinking about God and Jesus the Christ.
Paperback: 978-1-84694-937-1 ebook: 978-1-84694-938-8

Celtic Wheel of the Year
Tess Ward
An original and inspiring selection of prayers combining
Christian and Celtic Pagan traditions, and interweaving their
calendars into a single pattern of prayer for every morning
and night of the year.
Paperback: 978-1-90504-795-6

Christian Atheist
Belonging without Believing
Brian Mountford
Christian Atheists don't believe in God but miss him: especially
the transcendent beauty of his music, language, ethics, and
community.
Paperback: 978-1-84694-439-0 ebook: 978-1-84694-929-6

Compassion Or Apocalypse?
A Comprehensible Guide to the Thoughts of René Girard
James Warren
How René Girard changes the way we think about God and the
Bible, and its relevance for our apocalypse-threatened world.
Paperback: 978-1-78279-073-0 ebook: 978-1-78279-072-3

Diary Of A Gay Priest
The Tightrope Walker
Rev. Dr. Malcolm Johnson
Full of anecdotes and amusing stories, but the Church is still a
dangerous place for a gay priest.
Paperback: 978-1-78279-002-0 ebook: 978-1-78099-999-9

Do You Need God?
Exploring Different Paths to Spirituality Even For Atheists
Rory J.Q. Barnes
An unbiased guide to the building blocks of spiritual belief.
Paperback: 978-1-78279-380-9 ebook: 978-1-78279-379-3

The Gay Gospels
Good News for Lesbian, Gay, Bisexual, and Transgendered
People
Keith Sharpe
This book refutes the idea that the Bible is homophobic
and makes visible the gay lives and validated homoerotic

experience to be found in it.

Paperback: 978-1-84694-548-9 ebook: 978-1-78099-063-7

The Illusion of "Truth"
The Real Jesus Behind the Grand Myth
Thomas Nehrer

Nehrer, uniquely aware of Reality's integrated flow, elucidates Jesus' penetrating, often mystifying insights – exposing widespread religious, scholarly and skeptical fallacy.
Paperback: 978-1-78279-548-3 ebook: 978-1-78279-551-3

Do We Need God to be Good?
An Anthropologist Considers the Evidence
C.R. Hallpike

What anthropology shows us about the delusions of New Atheism and Humanism.
Paperback: 978-1-78535-217-1 ebook: 978-1-78535-218-8

Fingerprints of Fire, Footprints of Peace
A Spiritual Manifesto from a Jesus Perspective
Noel Moules

Christian spirituality with attitude. Fourteen provocative pictures, from Radical Mystic to Messianic Anarchist, that explore identity, destiny, values and activism.
Paperback: 978-1-84694-612-7 ebook: 978-1-78099-903-6

Readers of ebooks can buy or view any of these bestsellers by clicking on the live link in the title. Most titles are published in paperback and as an ebook. Paperbacks are available in traditional bookshops. Both print and ebook formats are available online.